For the Love of the Packers

An A-to-Z Primer for Packers Fans of All Ages

Written by Frederick C. Klein   Illustrated and designed by Mark Anderson

When asked to write the foreword for this book called *For the Love of the Packers*, I said "Okay, I'll be happy to do it, but since for me the Packers are synonymous with Vince Lombardi, it's him I want to write about."

For eight years, Vince Lombardi was the most important man in my life. I respected him as a coach, a leader, and, more importantly, as a friend. If I needed advice, I could talk to him. He was tougher on me than he was on most of the other players, but I needed that extra push.

I was very close to Lombardi, and the other players knew that. Whenever there was a problem on the team, the guys wanted me to go in and talk to him. They knew I could do this. But I never won an argument with him.

Lombardi's years with the Packers are still among the greatest achievements in sports. Five NFL championships and victories in the first two Super Bowls are standards nobody else has reached. He is a legend, the best example of a winner we have in America. I loved every minute I spent with him. He was a very special man and it was a time in my life I will treasure forever.

For the Love of the Packers? Sure, there's a lot to love, and this wonderfully unique book includes much of it, but my special love will always be reserved for the man I consider to be the greatest coach in the history of the NFL.

–Paul Hornung

"A" is for

Aldridge,

An end with no bend.
When he'd hit a runner he'd
Put him on the mend.

Lionel Aldridge came to the Packers in 1963 from Utah State University. He went on to become a fixture in their defensive line for nine seasons, including the championship years of 1965, 1966, and 1967. He was known for his durability and for his ability to both stop the run and rush the passer. He missed only three regular-season games during his career in Green Bay.

"B" is for

Brown,

Whose trademark was girth.
When he took the field
He rattled the earth.

Gilbert Brown was the prototypical nose tackle of the 1990s, a massive man who anchored the middle of the Packers' defensive line. **Nicknamed "the Grave Digger" for his dirt-shoveling charade after tackles,** he was listed as weighing 345 pounds, but many people thought he was heavier. So famous was his eating prowess that a Green Bay restaurant featured the "Gilbert Burger" in his honor. It contained double everything except pickles, which he didn't like.

"C" is for Canadeo,

The "Ghost" with the most.
Give him the ball and
He'd find the goal post.

Tony Canadeo went to little Gonzaga University in Spokane, Washington, where he got the nickname "the Gray Ghost of Gonzaga." Short but tough and elusive, he started variously at quarterback, running back, and defensive back in his 11 seasons with the Pack (1941–1944; 1946–1952). In 1949 he became the first Packer to rush for more than 1,000 yards. He registered 8,667 yards of total offense over his career.

"D" is for

Driver;

This wheelman can steer.
When Brett looked downfield,
There was Don in the clear!

Donald Driver was a late-round draft choice out of Alcorn State University in 1999, but after settling into the pro game he became an NFL star and Brett Favre's favorite pass receiver. Through 2007 the Houston, Texas, native was a four-time Pro Bowl selection and had exceeded the 1,000-yard receptions mark in five seasons. His 503 career catches put him third on the team's all-time list.

"E" is for

Earp,

Not Wyatt but "Jug."
At center for the Pack
He was a sparkplug.

Francis Louis "Jug" Earp was an athletic legend at Millikin University in Illinois, then starred in his 11 seasons in Green Bay (1922–1932). In the pros he played every line position, but mostly center. **He is credited with inventing the modern center snap,** where the crouching center, facing forward, hands the ball between his legs to the quarterback.

"**F**" is for

Favre,

A Mississippi lad,
In each Packers outing
He gave all that he had.

Brett Favre, from Kiln, Mississippi, was the Packers' offensive leader after taking over as starting quarterback in 1992 until his retirement after the 2007 season. His competitive spirit, durability, and all-out playing style made him the team's most popular player as well. Favre led the Packers to the Super Bowl XXXI championship in January 1997. **At the time of his retirement, he held NFL career records for most passing yards (61,655), most completions (5,377), and most touchdown passes (442)**, among others. His brilliant performance in leading the Pack to the 2007 NFC championship game, at age 38, earned him *Sports Illustrated* magazine's "Sportsman of the Year" award.

"G" is for Gregg;

As a lineman, the best.
When his playing days ended
He took the coaching test.

Forrest Gregg spent 14 seasons with the Packers and was a starting offensive tackle on all five of their 1960s championship teams. Not big for his position at 250 pounds, he instead overcame foes with superior technique and game preparation. He did this so well that he was named to the All-NFL team eight straight times (1960–1967), and Vince Lombardi called him "the finest player I ever coached." Gregg later turned to coaching himself, eventually holding the top job with the Cleveland Browns, Cincinnati Bengals, and the Packers (1984–1987), and with his alma mater, Southern Methodist University.

"H" is for Herber and Hutson,

An aerial show.
They racked up big yardage
And made the score grow.

Green Bay native **Arnie Herber was one of pro football's first great long passers**, and his throws helped usher in the modern passing game. He was a mainstay of the championship Pack teams of the 1930s. For much of that period his favorite receiver was end **Don Hutson, the best pass catcher of the NFL's first 50 years**. For many years the lean former University of Alabama star held the league record for touchdown receptions (99). More than 60 years after his 1945 retirement he still leads the team in career touchdowns (105) and stands third in catches (488) and yards gained receiving (7,991).

"I" is for Indian,

A firm that packed meat.
Its $500 for jerseys
Began the Pack beat.

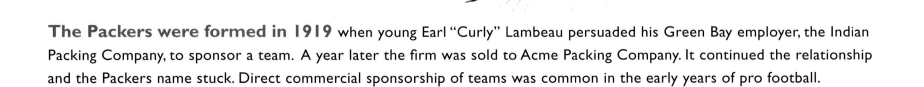

The Packers were formed in 1919 when young Earl "Curly" Lambeau persuaded his Green Bay employer, the Indian Packing Company, to sponsor a team. A year later the firm was sold to Acme Packing Company. It continued the relationship and the Packers name stuck. Direct commercial sponsorship of teams was common in the early years of pro football.

"J" is for Jordan,

Who was good on the mat. Then he came to Green Bay
And knocked running backs flat.

"K" is for Kramer,

Whose block cleared the way
for the big "Ice Bowl" victory
That's remembered today.

Henry Jordan was a multisport athlete at the University of Virginia, lettering in wrestling and track as well as in football. In 1957 he was runner-up in the heavyweight division of the national collegiate wrestling tournament. Jordan excelled as a defensive tackle with the Packers from 1959 through 1969, joining Willie Davis and Lionel Aldridge on one of the game's all-time best defensive lines. He is one of 10 members of the 1960s champions to be elected to the NFL's Hall of Fame.

Jerry Kramer played right guard on the 1960s Pack titleholders, winning fame as a lead blocker in the famous "Green Bay sweep." He gained further note as co-author of the book *Instant Replay*, his diary of the 1967 season that's considered a sports classic. Kramer's block that allowed quarterback Bart Starr to score the winning points on a 1-yard sneak in the dying seconds of the frigid "Ice Bowl" game against Dallas for the 1967 NFL crown provided one of football's most unforgettable moments.

"L" is for

Lambeau,

The man and the Field.
In Packerdom annals
No name's deeper sealed.

Few individuals have had a longer or more productive association with a major sports team than Earl "Curly" Lambeau. He founded the Packers in 1919, played for them for 11 seasons, and was their only head coach through 1949. His teams won six NFL championships and more than 200 games. City Stadium, the Packers' home since it was built in1957, was renamed Lambeau Field in his honor in 1965. His statue stands outside the structure.

"M" is for McNally,

Who played many a part.
His days on the gridiron
Were only a start.

John McNally wanted to play semi-pro football while still in college, so to protect his eligibility took the name "Johnny Blood" after a Rudolph Valentino movie (*Blood and Sand*) he enjoyed. As Blood he played 14 NFL seasons ending in 1938. Seven of them were in Green Bay, where he starred at halfback on four championship clubs. McNally pursued multiple interests after football. He was an Army cryptographer in World War II. At age 42 he returned to St. John's College in Minnesota, earned a degree in economics, and later taught the subject and wrote a textbook. He was said to take the stage and recite long verses from Shakespeare by heart. They made a movie that was based on his life and career called *Leatherheads* starring George Clooney.

"N" is for Nitschke,

Who fomented foe fear.
He pounced on a runner
Like a lion on a deer.

Ray Nitschke was a second-string fullback and sometime-linebacker at the University of Illinois who was switched to full-time defense in Green Bay. He won the team's starting middle linebacker job in 1960 and quickly became known for his tackling ferocity and swiftness of pursuit. **He was the Most Valuable Player of the Packers' 1962 NFL title game against the New York Giants and a many-time All-Pro, and was named to the league's 50-Year and 75th-Anniversary teams.**

"O" is for

Nothing,

Which is what the Giants got,
In two title games
When the Packers were hot.

In the NFL's long history only five championship playoff games have ended in shutouts, and the Pack recorded two of them. In 1939, at State Fair Park in Milwaukee, they beat the New York Giants 27–0 as Arnie Herber and Cecil Isbell each threw touchdown passes and the defense held the visitors to 164 yards. Twenty-two years later in Green Bay, they beat the New Yorkers by a 37–0 score. Paul Hornung scored 19 points in that one on a touchdown run, three field goals, and four extra points. The Pack defense secured the rout with four pass interceptions and a fumble recovery.

"P" is for Paul Hornung,

A man about town.
   He'd sweat for the Pack,
Then chug a few down.

Hornung was the last of the game's triple-threat backs in an increasingly specialized NFL. He was a quarterback at Notre Dame, where he passed, ran, and kicked so well that he won the 1956 Heisman Trophy with a team whose won-lost record was 2–8. He became a halfback in Green Bay, and seldom passed, but ran, caught, and kicked his way to league scoring titles in 1959, 1960, and 1961. Hornung was a "playboy" off the field as well. **"Never get married in the morning— you never know who you might meet that night,"** he said. He served a year's suspension for betting on sports, but returned to the Packers and later was elected to the league's Hall of Fame.

"Q" is for

Quarterback,

Where the Packers went far
With Isbell, Lynn Dickey,
And, most of all, Bart Starr.

Cecil Isbell took over as Packers tailback in 1938 but his duties were mostly those of a present-day quarterback. The possessor of a rifle arm and the man Curly Lambeau called the best passer he'd ever seen, he starred for the 1939 champs and in 1942 became the first Packer to throw for more than 2,000 yards. **Dickey** was the Pack quarterback from the mid-1970s to the mid-1980s, racking up big yardage with less-than-successful teams. **The cool-headed Starr came aboard in 1956 as a 17th-round draft choice** out of the University of Alabama and stuck around to command the great Packer dynasty squads. From 1975 through 1983 he was the team's head coach.

"R" is for

Remmel,

Who again and again
Served Packer fans
With paper and pen.

Lee Remmel has had a more-than-60-year association with the Packers—29 as a sportswriter and columnist for the *Green Bay Press-Gazette*, 30-plus more as the team's chief public relations officer, and lately as team historian. The well-liked native of Shawano, Wisconsin, is a member of the Packers Hall of Fame and the press box in Lambeau Field is named in his honor.

"S" is for

Sharpe,

Who honed his blade fine.
He'd gather a pass
And head for the line.

Sterling Sharpe was the Packers' first-round draft choice out of the University of South Carolina in 1988. He immediately became Green Bay's top receiver and held that distinction through each of his seven NFL seasons. Big and fast and with a nose for the goal, Sharpe holds team records for career receptions (595) and touchdown catches in a season (18 in 1994), and is second in yards gained receiving (8,134) despite his relatively short career. After a neck injury ended his playing days he became a television analyst for NFL games.

"T" is for

Taylor,

Also for Tank.
This hard-driving fullback
Put points in the bank.

Jim Taylor is the Pack's all-time leading rusher with 8,207 yards gained over his nine seasons (1958–66) in Green Bay. In that span he scored 99 touchdowns, a total second only to the great Don Hutson's 105 in the team's record book. A low-to-the-ground fullback from Louisiana, Taylor was the Pack's bread-and-butter runner, regularly called upon in short-yardage situations for first downs or touchdowns. He was an excellent blocker as well.

"U" is for Umpire,

Cal Hubbard by name.
Plaques in two famous shrines
Attest to his fame.

At 6'5" and 250 pounds, Robert "Cal" Hubbard was an imposing figure in pro football's early days, a two-way tackle without peer on either side of the ball. He starred on the Packers championship teams of 1929, 1930, and 1931. After he left football he became a big-league baseball umpire, calling games from 1936 through 1951 and serving as the American League's umpire supervisor for 16 years after that. He is the only person to be elected to both the baseball and NFL halls of fame.

"V" is for Vince,

Who cracked a mean whip.
He had only one goal:
The championship.

Vince Lombardi became the Packers' head coach in 1958 after a term as offensive coordinator of the New York Giants. A disciplinarian with little patience for failure, he immediately put the team on "Lombardi Time," meaning that everything started 10 or 15 minutes before it was scheduled to begin. Some players chafed under his stern reign. **"He treats us all the same—like dogs,"** said Henry Jordan. But the team responded with an unprecedented run of five NFL titles in seven years (1961, 1962, 1965–1967), including victories in the first two Super Bowls. Lombardi never had a losing season in his nine years at the Green Bay helm.

"W" is for White,

A collector of sacks.
He'd flick off the blockers
And mash the quarterbacks.

Reggie White was one of football's greatest defensive linemen, a big, skilled athlete who turned the quarterback sack into his signature play. Nicknamed the "Minister of Defense" because he also was an ordained clergyman, he starred with the Philadelphia Eagles for eight seasons before joining the Packers as a free agent in 1993. He gilded his legend in Wisconsin by helping the Pack win Super Bowl XXXI. **When he retired in 2000 he was the NFL's all-time sack leader with 198.**

"X" is a mark
Coaches make in their books.
The Pack has given plenty
Of those guys a look.

Green Bay has had many notable coaches besides Lambeau and Lombardi. **Dan Devine**, who'd previously coached at Notre Dame, guided the team for four seasons (1971–1974) and led it into the 1972 playoffs. **Mike Holmgren** won two-thirds of his games and the 1996 Super Bowl during his seven-year tenure (1992–1998). **Mike Sherman's** teams gained the playoffs with 12–4 regular-season records in 2001 and 2002. The current head coach, **Mike McCarthy**, is an offensive specialist who came on board in 2006 promising to return the Pack attack to the level of its glory days. He's followed through on the pledge, posting an 8–8 record in his first season and going 14–4 the next and guiding the team to the NFC championship game.